Published by McNaughty Books, an imprint of John Napir Ltd
P.O.Box 3353. London N.1. 1SR.

Design by Niamh Lehane.
Photographs:- Earl Farquhar © Illustrated London News Picture Library. Edwina Currie © Magi Haroun / Today Newspaper. Harvey Proctor and Pamela Bordes © Rex Features Ltd. Alan Clark © UPP. All others © The Press Association Ltd.

ISBN 1-898 505 047
Printed and bound in the E.E.C.

McNaughty Books

THE McTORY BOOK OF BONKS!

Written & Compiled by Norman ffamily-Values
Illustrated by Themselves

CONTENTS

INTRODUCTION

> "It's hypocritical to expect people under tremendous pressure to behave impeccably. Whom you sleep with on a Saturday night has nothing to do with how well you do your job.I don't think any the less of David because he had an undignified fling with a six foot actress"

Edwina Currie on David Mellor

When Farquhar McNaughty asked me to compile this McTory Book of Bonks I protested.

It seems to me that most women find power very attractive, and if some have succeeded on occasions in luring Politicians into indiscretions it would be most unfair to blame the Politicians. (I don't believe we blame flies for getting caught in spiders' webs).

So, what with my initial distaste, and my natural laziness, I wrote to thirty of the relevant Politicians asking for a witty 250 words and offering to pay £250 to charity for each contribution used. Teresa Gorman and Alan Clark had the decency to reply that they couldn't help. John Major's contribution is included, Jeffrey Archer's isn't (nice try Jeff). None of the rest bothered to reply, so I've had to write all the entries myself.

All the information contained in this book has been gleaned from Press reports and other published sources. Where I've found printed reports to have been later retracted I've stated so. However should any statements be incorrect I unreservedly apologise.

Norman ffamily-Values

SPOT THE BALLS COMPETITION

The Palace of Westminster

1. This competition is only open to MPs or former MPs, their mistresses, male lovers or their private secretaries.
2. Using your skill and judgement place an X on the position of your choice.
3. In the case of MPs and former MPs, deny strenuously that you ever did so.
4. My decision will be biased and all correspondence may be forwarded to a National Newspaper and/or Max Clifford.
5. There's another competition for the rest of you on page 28.

POKIN' IN THE PALACE

Pokin' in the Palace is a peculiarly English way of ending a political career. It has a long tradition. Indeed historians generally agree that it can be traced back as far as Edward II, whose political career ended rather abruptly when he found a red hot poker up his bum.

These days, Pokin' in the Palace is usually conducted in a Front to Basics position, although there is considerable public support for reverting to the original Back to Basics Edward II method, at least as far as Tory MPs are concerned.

In the current version, the method has six stages:-

- exposed MP
- MP exposed
- Max Clifford
- her description of the Palace location used
- MP's denial
- end of political career

BONKING TORIES

John Profumo collects his C.B.E.

JOHN PROFUMO
ex TORY MP
Stratford on Avon

Every decent political scandal needs four elements:

- a senior member of government.
- sex, preferably with call-girls.
- public denials followed by admission, resignation and humiliation.
- possible security breaches.

The possible security breach element preferably requires that the politician is responsible for some part of National Security and that the sexual partner is a member of, or having another affair with, Public Enemy No 1. In the Seventeenth Century, Public Enemy No.1 meant a Roman Catholic, during the First and Second World Wars it meant a German, in the 1950's and 1960's a Russian, and since the 1970's an Arab, preferably Libyan, P.L.O. or Iraqi.

John Profumo scored a bulls eye. He was a Privy Counsellor, Secretary of State for War, he had an affair with Christine Keeler and denied it in the House of Commons, before admitting it and resigning. Christine Keeler also knew Captain Ivanov a Russian Embassy Security Officer. Every ingredient was there.

Except that probably it wasn't. There had been no security breach and Christine Keeler was more a fun-time girl than a prostitute - no-one now suggests that he ever paid her. And Profumo wasn't even in the Cabinet. Much was made of lieing to Parliament but, as William Waldegrave recently pointed out, there are times when it's necessary. If the same facts occurred today, Profumo would still be an M.P., and before the Back to Basics campaign might even have kept his Government job.

The two saddest aspects of the affair are the suicide of Stephen Ward and the fact that Profumo has yet to get the life peerage he deserves. (q.v. The Virgin Queen).

VISCOUNT LAMBTON
ex TORY MP
Berwick on Tweed

Viscount Lambton was the heir to the Earl of Durham but disclaimed the title when he inherited it in 1970 so that he could remain an MP. By the age of 50 he had become in effect the Air Minister when, in 1972, he got involved with a call-girl ring.

One of the girls, Norma Levy, got mixed up with a man with a criminal record, feared Lambton might be blackmailed, and made certain that the government knew. Viscount Lambton duly resigned.

In the report on the affair the Permanent Security Commission reported that when at Norma's flat, in the company of prostitutes, he had smoked cannabis and he was subsequently fined £300 for doing so. Since then, apart from enjoying his vast wealth, he has written biographies. His daughter recently appeared as Miss Whiplash in the 1986 film "Sid and Nancy".

EARL JELLICOE

Earl Jellicoe was most unfortunate. At the time of the Viscount Lambton scandal he volunteered to the Prime Minister, Edward Heath, the information that he had occasionally used call-girls Being an honourable man, he offered to resign from the Government.

Most surprisingly, given that there had been no public scandal, Edward Heath accepted his offer. It is doubtful that The Virgin Queen would have taken such a purist stand, but given that Earl Jellicoe was at the time a member of the Cabinet, there were potential security implications. Memories of the Profumo scandal which had crippled the previous Tory Macmillan government were also fresh in everybody's mind.

Sir Nicholas finds a tick

SIR NICHOLAS FAIRBAIRN
TORY MP
Perth & Kinross

Nicholas Fairbairn, like Alan Clark and Chris Smith, has been remarkably frank about his hobbies, although in Fairbairn's case they keep changing. In 1973 his main interests were reportedly making love, ends meet and people laugh. Having divorced his wife of 17 years in 1979 (hobby of the year:- upholding what's right and demolishing what's left), he started an affair with a House of Commons secretary, Pamela Milne.

Shortly before Christmas 1981 (hobby of the year:- the cure and eradication of British Tick fever), it was reported that Pamela had been found hanging from a lamp-post outside his London flat. She denied this although admitting to attempting suicide. In an article she was reported as saying that Nicholas called her his "Ant" and his ex-wife "Old Hoarfrost". Nicholas subsequently remarried and now reportedly spends his free time drawing ships, making quips, confounding whips and scuttling drips.

Like other males keen on love-making his advances have not always been successful. When attacking a clause in a female MP's kerb-crawling Bill, Sir Nicholas was reported as saying that he had always been attracted to her, and she to have replied that sleeping with a dead cod would have been preferable.

Cecil searches for the toothpaste tube

From 1979 to 1982 he was Solicitor General for Scotland. His divorce, the non-existant lamp-post, his changing hobbies and dead cod had no effect on his position, though he did have to resign when he commented on a Glasgow rape case outside Parliament.

CECIL PARKINSON
ex TORY MP
Hertsmere

It has been reported that one of Cecil Parkinson's favourite quotations was the Richard Nixon comment "You cannot put the toothpaste back in the tube". Unfortunately he forgot it when having an affair with his former secretary Sarah Keays.

In October 1983, when she was 6 months pregnant with his child, Cecil made their affair public. Initially, with the support of The Virgin Queen, he hoped to brazen it out but ten days later had to resign. Their child was born on 31st December 1983.

At the time he was a Cabinet Minister and Secretary of State for Trade and Industry. However fortune smiled, and by 1987 he was back in the Cabinet and got a life peerage in 1992.

DAVID MELLOR
TORY MP
Putney

Farquhar McNaughty and myself had many arguments over whether David Mellor should be in the "Bonking Tories" section or the "Slightly Sleazy?" section, because despite his bonki bits he probably would have survived as a Minister if it hadn't been for his slightly sleazy bits. In the end we compromised. Mellor once claimed "I am strongly flavoured, I am the political equivalent of a curry". Now we all know that curries have many spicy bits so we've split the ingredients - bonki bits here, slightly sleazy under "Slightly Sleazy?", and Antonia de Sancha under the "Bevy of Beauties".

The bonki bit story is quite simple. David Mellor, the then Secretary of State for National Heritage (Minister for Fun), probably started having an affair with actress Antonia de Sancha around June'92. She was having trouble paying her rent and told a certain Mr Philp of her financial position and the fact that she was seeing a politician. Philp said he was going abroad and offered her his flat having previously bugged the phone. He then sold the story to The People who, despite the debate then going on about press-intrusion into people's private lives, published it.

The People justified the report as Mellor had mentioned in one telephone call that he was so "seriously knackered" after a night of bonki bits that he was having trouble concentrating on his speech writing. When all was revealed David Mellor offered to resign but John Major refused. It was July, his wife stood by him, and Parliament was not sitting. He might have got away with it. Why he did not, is told on pages 38 - 41.

STEPHEN NORRIS
TORY MP
Epping Forest

Stephen Norris went to George Harrison's and Paul McCartney's old school in Liverpool. Whilst there he met Edwina Currie who is reported to have said "He tried it on for six weeks when I was 17 but it got him nowhere... Women like him because he is kind, warm and funny". Lots of women like him apparently.

Stephen married in 1969 the daughter of an Admiral and niece of Cardinal Basil Hume. He is a self-made millionaire in the car trade, and his marriage palled - no chance of a divorce as his wife is a strict Roman Catholic.

So the affairs started. First there was Clare Marx, a surgeon, then there was Lynn Taylor, a sales executive, then Sheila Gunn, a Times journalist, then Emma Courtney, a House of Commons secretary, then Jennifer Sharp, a Director of Harpers and Queen, then.....

As one of them reportedly remarked “He simply called us all ‘Darling’, so if he couldn’t remember our names at any time he was covered”.

The affairs dribbled out into the Press fairly slowly from the Summer of 1993. When three were known, a senior Tory remarked “Having one mistress may be regarded as a misfortune. Three is breaking new ground”. Five presumably is a major tunnelling job.

The surprise is that he survived the 1993 Tory Party Conference and the whole Back to Basics row to remain a Transport Minister. How did he do it ? The secret I suspect is twofold. Firstly he was genuinely liked by colleagues, the women, and his wife. Secondly perhaps there is safety in numbers. A mistress a day, keeps the tabloids at bay ?

TIM YEO
TORY MP
Suffolk South

Tim Yeo was the first in a series of political downfalls following the launch of the Back to Basics campaign. John Major had intended that the campaign should concentrate people’s minds on achieving good basic standards in Education, Health Care etc, a political reaction from the fashionable concepts of the 1970s.

Stephen with an unfortunate number plate

However it was not long before Back to Basics was hijacked as a campaign for family values and against supposedly "irresponsible" single mothers who allegedly were more likely to produce criminal children and cost the State vast sums of money in social security and housing payments.

Tim Yeo had in the past led campaigns to publicise the case of thalidomide children and was a former Director of the Spastics Society. In December 1993 he was a Minister of State at the Department of the Environment. However on one occasion he had been reported as saying "It is in everyone's interest to reduce broken families and the number of single parents".

On Christmas Eve 1993 the story broke that he had a five month old daughter by a Hackney Tory Councillor. Being Christmas, Mr Yeo went off on holiday to the Seychelles with his family. On his return the gentlemen of the Press were at him to resign. He thought not. However after his admission of another illegitimate child the Vice-Chairman of one of his constituency branches commented "I am very disappointed by our M.P. and strongly believe he should resign his ministerial position". He had to.

The Hackney Tory Councillor, Julia Stent, appeared a month later in a seven page spread in Hello! magazine. It was alleged at the time that £50,000 was the going rate of pay to celebrities.

GARY WALLER
TORY MP
Keighley

In January 1994 The People newspaper revealed that the unmarried 48 year old Gary Waller had a six year old love-child by a House of Commons secretary Fay Stockwell. Nothing wrong with that - only two problems. His current girl-friend apparently thought they had been going out together for nine years so the maths didn't add up. And Mr Waller had temporary amnesia and denied the story for a few days.

Pictured on the front of a National Newspaper wearing a T'shirt emblazoned "Tories do it better" was unfortunate, but temporary amnesia - surely that's a requirement for Politicians.

In essence though, it was all a bit stupid and a year earlier would hardly have rated a one-line mention. Like David Ashby he just seems to have been a victim of the Back to Basics media witch-hunt.

NOT BONKING TORIES

NICHOLAS SOAMES
TORY MP
Crawley

Nicholas Soames is not famous for his bonki bits - he's famous for another indulgence - food. As a Founder Member of the Westminster Dining Club, "Bunters" or "Nickers", as the Junior Agricultural Minister is known, varies between 16 and 20 stone. "I am the Minister of Food... and it's not my job to sit there looking as if I eat bat's droppings". Instead he is constantly chewing toffees and claims that his old childhood friend Prince Charles makes the best bread and butter pudding he has ever eaten.

Renowned , like his father, for his sense of humour and generally regarded by all (even Dennis Skinner q.v.) as a genuinely good bloke, readers may well ask what he's doing in a book like this. Well, he wins his entry for his famous definition of Back to Basics made when presenting awards for wild game conservation:-

Nickers persues his indulgence

"I'll tell you what Back to Basics means. It's that wonderful combination - champagne, shooting and conservation. If we had a bit more of those, and a bit less of the other, we'd all be in better shape".

HARTLEY BOOTH
TORY MP
Finchley

At the height of the Back to Basics storm poor Hartley was exposed as having had an affair with a former House of Commons researcher. At first nobody suggested, and he denied, any bonking and clearly an "orgasmic situation" had never arisen. Not much of an affair.

But the Press had a great time. She was a left-wing 22 year old former art model who had posed nude for drawing classes at £5 per hour. He was a "Campaigner for the Family" Methodist Lay Preacher who had written her love poems. He had earlier written nonsense rhymes to his wife under the name Justin Thyme but his thyming on this occasion was appalling. He resigned from his job as P.P.S. to Foreign Office Minister Douglas Hogg It was reported that after the "affair" started he had tried to stop, but even a priest couldn't pray him out of it.

EDWINA CURRIE
TORY MP
Derbyshire South

Edwina Currie is an extremely successful self-publicist - in fact someone remarked that she made Jeffrey Archer look like a recluse. Happily married, she has always managed to present herself as slightly naughty.

In 1981 at a Tory Party Conference as she brandished handcuffs at the Home Secretary, the watching Arts Minister Lord Gowrie is said to have experienced "a bat's squeak of desire". (Tory Ministers seem to be into bats, see Nicholas Soames)

Appointed by The Virgin Queen as Junior Health Minister she kept in the Press with her comments on how the old should keep warm (wear Long Johns), on the dreadfulness of the Northern diet, and on how businessmen could avoid getting Aids on overseas trips (take along the wife, or a good book). She even appeared on T.V. to give a demonstration (with her hands) as to how to put on a condom, and apparently once returned a shipment of condoms to Japan as they were too small.

However, after her comment that most of the country's

egg-production was affected by salmonella she had to resign.Undaunted by Chickengate, Eggwina, as she was dubbed, still managed to get reported. There was the libel action against the Observer in which she won £5000, revealing under questioning from George Carmen QC, that she kept suspenders in her wardrobe but not revealing whether she ever wore them. There was the review of The Joy of Sexual Fantasy "Terms such as 'member's entrance' certainly took on a new meaning". And then there was the satisfying incident of emptying a glass of orange juice over the head of a Labour MP after a T.V. interview. "I enjoyed that, I have wanted to do that for a long time".

In 1992, having refused a Ministerial post under John Major, she got a reported £100,000 advance for an unwritten book "A Parliamentary Affair". This caused quite a stir on publication as a portcullis was displayed on a girl's leg on the cover.

A fiesty lass, and a leader of the campaign to reduce legal homosexual consent to 16, but one of the few MPs who don't go in for hypocrisy. Whilst many MPs preach family values and practice playing away, she practices family values and sympathises with other's mistakes

One of the few good eggs?

Anyone for tennis?

DEFINITELY NOT BONKING TORIES

As I mentioned in my introduction I did try to get MPs to write their own entries. I wrote to them asking for two hundred and fifty words on a particular subject and promising £250 for their reply.
Some of the subjects set were:-

Alan Clark - erogenous zones
Jeffrey Archer - bouncing back
David Ashby - weekend breaks
John Major - Back to Basics
Tim Yeo - Fathers of the House
Nicholas Fairbairn - himself
David Mellor - frolics and football

I suppose I have to admit that some of the subjects were a bit difficult. But I was most surprised that John Major wasn't able to think of two hundred and fifty words on Back to Basics.

The cleverest and only witty reply came from Jeffrey Archer, but Farquhar McNaughty has refused to publish it because our Jeff wanted a contribution of considerably more than £250 payable to the Tory Party for the rights.

Farquhar thinks we've all paid the Tories enough, and I confess I'm inclined to agree. So, on pages 30 and 31, I have printed my initial letter to Jeffrey and my response to his reply. Readers are asked to supply suggestions as to the letter in-between. The best suggestion will win £250 and I'll publish it in a future edition, - Farquhar willing!

10 DOWNING STREET
LONDON SW1A 2AA

From the Correspondence Secretary 25 April 1994

Dear Mr Ffamily-Values

The Prime Minister has asked me to thank you for your recent letter. I regret that this is not a matter in which Mr Major can help you.

Yours sincerely,

Mrs P Wilkinson

Norman ffamily-Values

Lord Archer

19th April 1994

Alembic House
93 Albert Embankment
London
SE1 7TY

Dear Lord Archer,

I am writing to ask for your help.

In a moment of temporary insanity I'm afraid I accepted Farquhar McNaughty's offer to write the McTory Book of Bonks.

It seems to me that the only way to approach the subject is in a humorous rather than a moralistic or nasty vein so I've created a number of general headings:

- Bonking Tories
- Not Bonking Tories
- Definitely Not Bonking Tories
- Bonking But Not Tory
- Playful Members
- Gay Young Bachelors

You may not be over-gruntled to know that I've pencilled in an entry for you but I'm stuck - writers block I suppose. How to write the entry ? Which section ?

In the circumstances I wondered if I could persuade you to write your own entry - it needs to be only around 250 words. Indiscretions, anecdotes, absurdities etc on the general theme of "Bouncing Back" would be most welcome as would any photos.

Despite his well-documented (and well deserved) reputation as a miser, Farquhar has most kindly offered to donate £250 to your chosen charity for any material used.

As I mentioned this is all a great mistake on my part, but then we are all capable of minor lapses in judgement, I suppose...

Kind regards

Norman ff-V

N.ff.V.

Norman ffamily-Values

Lord Archer

26th April 1994

Alembic House
93 Albert Embankment
London
SE1 7TY

Dear Jeff

Trouble, Trouble.

I showed your letter to Farquhar McNaughty and he exploded. You see there is the small matter of his distant relative, the notorious gay Earl Farquhar, who embezzled £20,000 when Treasurer of the Tory Party in 1922 - he thinks you're trying to get it back.

Eventually I calmed him down but I still couldn't get him to budge. His final comment was "Not a penny more, Not a penny less" which struck me as quite a good title for a book.

So I'm afraid it's £250 or nothing. Sorry.

Kind regards

Norman ffamily-Values

P.S. D'you think the McLoony Book of Lefties would have any mileage.

NORMAN LAMONT
TORY MP
Kingston upon Thames

Norman Lamont is best described as accident prone. Although much reported as "a bit of a flirt" no-one has ever suggested he went any further. Even his famous statement "Birds are a wonderful soothing thing" apparently referred to the feathery types.

He first ran into trouble when as a Junior Minister in 1985 he "walked into a wall" and got a black eye. Unfortunately, the wall, in the shape of an art dealer, claimed later that he had inflicted the injury after finding Lamont late one night in the house of Lord Forte's daughter. Lamont described the incident as "innocent but complicated". The Virgin Queen took no notice; others said it was Lamontable.

As The Virgin Queen's reign came to an end, Lamont found himself as Chief Secretary to the Treasury and borrowing the Gayfere Street house of Alan Duncan q.v., ran a successful campaign for John Major. He was rewarded with the job as Chancellor.

Then things started to go wrong. The first problem was the revelation that his house had been rented out to Sara Dale, a £90 per hour Miss Whiplash. Not Lamont's fault as he had employed estate agents and how was he to know. More important, how to get her out. "Crack the whip", suggested Dennis Skinner. But Lamont used lawyers. In 1992 it emerged that the costs of getting rid of Miss Whiplash had been nearly £23,000 of which £4,700 had been paid from public funds, and the balance from an anonymous benefactor.

The second problem was the publication in November 1992 of the fact that in the previous eight years Lamont had been over his Access limit no fewer than twenty-two times. Not bad for a Chancellor.

Third came the totally false report that he had bought cheap champagne and a packet of Raffles cigarettes at a Threshers off-licence in Paddington late one night. The Threshers manager who made up the story was later deported on a first-class seat back to Nigeria.

By early 1993 Lamont was being ridiculed constantly in the Press. His monthly visions of green shoots of recovery, which usually turned out to be the figment of his advisors' imagination didn't help. Neither did the E.R.M. fiasco.

Then, just before the Newbury by-election he made his infamous comment "Je ne regrette rien". John Major finally put him out of his misery.

JEFFREY ARCHER
ex TORY MP
Louth

Jeffrey Archer, like Norman Lamont, has proved rather accident prone in his political career, but far more resilient.

After being President of Oxford University Athletic Club and running for England he became the youngest MP when elected in 1969.

Generally regarded as a man with a great future, he unfortunately invested £400,000 of borrowed money in a Canadian venture which proved to be fraudulent. Facing bankruptcy, he resigned his seat and in ten weeks wrote "Not a penny more, not a penny less" which launched his hugely successful writing career.

A tireless worker for the Tory Party, by 1985 he had been appointed Deputy Chairman when disaster struck for the second time. Monica Coghlan a confessed prostitute was told by a solicitor friend of hers that the customer she had just seen was Jeffrey Archer. The newspapers got involved and Monica made a series of pleading calls to Jeffrey. As she was obviously being harassed, he gave her some money (£2,000) so that she and her ten year old son could go abroad for a while. The phone calls had been taped and the money transaction photographed by the News of the World. The story was published and Jeffrey had to resign.

In a series of famous libel actions Jeffrey picked up £500,000 for false suggestions in some papers that he had ever used Monica's services, and then donated the money to charity.

Typically he bounced back, and in 1992 was created Lord Archer.

JOHN MAJOR
TORY MP
Huntingdon

In 1993 the New Statesman published an article about the false rumours flying around about a supposed affair between John Major, the Prime Minister, and Clare Latimer. Clare owned Clare's Kitchen, a catering company which many Ministers used to provide food and drink for functions.

As the New Statesman's article stated, despite the fact that these rumours were flying around, there was absolutely no substance to them. John Major was furious with the article and sued. He eventually settled for a payment of £1001.

The case is interesting in that it shows the problems Politicians face. A false rumour can start and gather momentum and there is little the Politician can do. Putting out a statement that the rumour is untrue (as Richard Gere and Cindy Crawford did) only draws attention to it. Ignoring it is always a possibility, but the slow drip of scandal can be very distressing emotionally both to the Politician, his family and any other parties supposedly involved. If an article is published stating that the rumour is false, the Politician can again ignore it, but if he sues, anyone can then legally comment on the fact that he has sued and why. A truly Catch 22 situation.

DAVID ASHBY

TORY MP

Leicestershire North-West

Shortly before Christmas 1993 Mr Ashby left his Italian wife Silvana and went to stay with a male chum Dr Kilduff. Apparently she pitched up and was ejected after the police were called - just a normal little marital tiff.

After Christmas David Ashby and a chum went on holiday together to France and to save money shared a Queen-sized bed in a French hotel. His reported retort "I've been all over the bloody place and shared bloody beds. Christ Almighty!" Quite so. Indeed some newspapers wrongly suggested a hotel in Goa.

He probably wasn't helped by the report that earlier in 1993 he had negotiated an agreement with Labour Members on the House of Commons Select Committee on Home Affairs whereby he would support an enquiry into Party Political Funding in return for their supporting an enquiry into lowering the age of homosexual consent. Why should this have been at all relevant ? No-one suggested that Edwina Currie qv., who led the campaign for the age to be lowered to 16, was a drag artiste.

Quite frankly, lots of innuendo and nothing happening

SLIGHTLY SLEAZY?

DAVID MELLOR
TORY MP
Putney

On pages 16 and 55 we tell the story of Mellor's bonki bits but it was the slightly sleazy bits which did him.

In September 1990 after Iraq had invaded Kuwait, The People Newspaper had revealed that David Mellor, then the Chief Secretary to the Treasury had accepted a holiday invitation to Marbella from Mona Bauwens. Mrs Bauwens had paid for the air tickets for Mellor, his wife and two children and paid the rent for the $20,000 per month villa. The People felt this inappropriate because Mona Bauwens father was the P.L.O. paymaster and the P.L.O. were supporting Saddam Hussein.

Mona Bauwens sued The People for libel. She personally had nothing to do with the P.L.O. and her father had only joined the P.L.O. when Yasser Arafat publicly renounced violence.

The Minister plays with a virgin

Following the De Sancha sex scandal in July'92, the Daily Mail revealed on September 10th 1992 that Mellor was friendly with a property dealer who had lent him a car and chauffeur, and a Mayfair flat where, allegedly, he had bonked De Sancha

Mellor had also introduced the developer to the Chairman of Chelsea football ground, and the developer and the Chairman had done a deal.

On September 17th 1992 the Bauwens libel case opened. George Carmen QC, representing The People, made the classic comment that Mellor had behaved like an ostrich who buried his head in the Marbella sand, thereby exposing his thinking part.This did Mellor's image no good at all.

The jury's split decision on September 20th left Mellor indeed exposed and when, on September 24th, details of another expenses paid holiday for the Mellor family in Abu Dhabi emerged, this time paid for the ruling Sheikh, Mellor had to resign as a Minister.

Although, as one paper remarked, he went from "Toe Job to No Job", he has since kept himself fully occupied as a journalist and a T.V. personality.

DAME SHIRLEY PORTER
ex TORY
Westminster Councillor

"I am minded to find as a fact that the electoral advantage of the majority party was the driving force behind the policy of increased designated sales. My provisional view is that the council was engaged in gerrymandering, which I am minded to find is a disgraceful and improper purpose and not a purpose for which a local authority may act."

District Auditor John Magill
Preliminary Report on
Tory-run Westminster Council
January 1994

His recommendation:- that ten people be ordered to pay back £21.25 million and banned from holding office as councillors.

Among the ten:- Dame Shirley Porter (allegedly worth £21 million) and Barry Legg (now Tory MP for Milton Keynes S.W)

KEITH BEST
ex TORY MP
Anglesey

Keith Best has had an interesting political career. After being nearly killed in a car crash in 1980, he came to the fore in 1986 with the political initiative of the twentieth century - the campaign to get Tiddliwinks sponsored financially by the Government. Unfortunately, during the British Telecom floatation he fraudulently made multiple applications. He was sentenced to four months in jail and a £3000 fine, reduced on appeal to a simple fine of £4500. After this brush with the law he became Chairman of Prisoners Abroad and in 1993 got the £30,000 job of Director of the Immigrants Appeals Advisory Service. Interestingly, early in his life he was briefly a school teacher and taught Robert Maxwell's two sons Kevin and Ian. Funny how life turns out.

ALAN DUNCAN
TORY MP
Rutland & Melton

Alan Duncan is a very kind chap. After becoming a millionaire from oil trading he secured the ultra-safe Tory seat at Rutland and set off on his political career. Sensibly debunking political correctness (he is reportedly fond of golliwogs) he discovered that his Westminster neighbour, a 78 year old, was living in a "grotty smelly revolting little pit". Duncan lent him £140,000 to buy it from the Council and did it up for him. Three years later Duncan owned the house now worth £300,000 and the old aged pensioner lived there rent-free. So what?

In another act of kindness Duncan's own house was used as John Major's headquarters as Mr Back to Basics himself campaigned for the Tory Party leadership. Shortly before Christmas 1993 Alan Duncan was made P.P.S. to the Health Minister Brian Mawhinney. He only kept the job three weeks as the Press found out about his little property deal.

Caught ski-ing shortly afterwards Alan reportedly remarked "At least if I'd been f.....g someone I'd have been enjoying myself."

TERESA GORMAN
TORY MP
Billericay

Poor Teresa Gorman got caught up in the Duncan problem when it was reported that between 1977-1982 she had bought two adjoining Westminster council houses for £55,000 and sold one off in 1993 for £455,000. After the costs of doing them up, inflation etc can she really have made much profit ?

BONKING BUT NOT TORY

JOHN STONEHOUSE

ex LABOUR MP
Walsall North

John Stonehouse was a Labour MP who held a number of posts in the first two Wilson governments from 1964 to 1970 rising from being P.P.S. to Roy Jenkins (then the Minister of Aviation) to Postmaster General and finally Minister of Posts and Communications.

In 1968 he was made a Privy Counsellor, but he never made the Cabinet. This may have been due to his mis-handling of the Post Office re-organisation (he was the professed socialist who introduced first and second class post). Or it may have been due to the fact that a Czech defector fingered him as a Czechoslovakian spy, although, in the event, he was cleared.

After he lost his government job in the 1970 General Election when the Tory Party won, he set up a number of businesses with his Parliamentary secretary Sheila Buckley with whom, sometime later, he started an affair. Although the businesses were grandly named (The British Bangladesh Trust, The London Capital Group, and Connoisseurs of Claret Ltd, to name a few) they were not very successful, and by 1974 both he and his companies were seriously in debt, him personally to the tune of £729,000.

Having taken out some £125,000 worth of life insurance policies payable to his wife in the event of his death, he flew to Miami, faked a drowning accident, and, using two false passports fled to Australia. At first everyone was fooled, but the Australian police were suspicious that he might be Lord Lucan and he was arrested. Both his wife and Sheila Buckley flew out to be with him.

He is said to have remarked "this story has everything, sex, politics, spies, big business, fraud and faked death". However it was the cheque and insurance frauds which did him and he was sentenced to 7 years in jail. Whilst in jail, his wife divorced him, and he later married Sheila Buckley. He now writes thrillers.

Somehow, though, after the revelations involving another one-time Labour M.P., Robert Maxwell, it all seems rather tawdry - now if Maxwell were found living in Australia, that would be a story.

Cap'n Bob
ex Labour MP - Buckingham
Is he really down-under?

DENNIS SKINNER

LABOUR MP

Bolsover

Dennis Skinner had for years enjoyed the reputation as a died in the wool political virgin. He never went on foreign trips, or drank in Commons bars, or allowed any journalist to buy him a drink or a meal. He claimed "You can't have half principles."

He was also famous for his one-liners. He called John Gummer "a little squirt" and was ordered from the House, he once shouted "Stop playing with yourself" at Cecil Parkinson qv. and famously agreed to withdraw only the word "pompous" after calling Dr David Owen "a pompous sod".

In February 1994 though he was caught having an affair with a House of Commons researcher who had a flat in Carlyle Square in Chelsea, and was photographed arriving there disguised in a muffler. All the MPs he had taunted had a field-day that the ultimate proletarian should have been caught exposing his principles in Chelsea.

The Beast of Bolsover became the Beast of Legover and took his seat to cries of "Where's your muffler ?" and "Chelsea! Chelsea!"

PADDY ASHDOWN
LIBERAL DEMOCRAT MP
Yeovil

In 1986, before he became leader of the Liberal Democrat Party, Paddy Ashdown employed Tricia Howard as his private secretary for eighteen months. He had a short affair with her. End of story.

Shortly before the 1992 election there was a break-in at the offices of his solicitors and the papers obtained were offered to the National Newspapers for £30,000. Paddy got an injunction in England but, as the Scottish papers were about to publish news on the affair, he decided to call a press conference and make a public statement. John Major reportedly phoned to offer his support.

One National Newspaper came up with the famous headline "It's Paddy Pantsdown". But the British Public reacted so superbly to his honesty, that Paddy Ashdown's poll-ratings went up sharply and the headline should have been "It's Polls Up for Pantsdown".

Sometime later a certain Mr Berkowitz was convicted of handling stolen papers and it emerged that he had previously been convicted of 230 offences of burglary, mostly from solicitors' offices, and had received jail sentences totalling 21 years over a period of 16 years. Curious

Paddy Ashdown's handling of the matter ought to have been used as a blueprint as to how to handle these things, but it seems few Politicians have learnt.

RON BROWN
ex LABOUR MP
Edinburgh Leith

Ron Brown had a short but colourful career in the Commons. Initially he had some problems with the Mace (the Parliamentary one, not the anti-rape spray).

Things got worse when he was alleged to have had an affair with a lady he met when she was working as a secretary to the Select Committee on Education. At the beginning of 1990 there were rumours of an M.P. having sex in House of Commons showers. "Yes it was us" said she, "No it wasn't" said he. Then there was the trip to Libya as a guest of Colonel Gaddafi.

Oh yes, and then he was fined £1000 for smashing up his mistress's flat after she ditched him, but he was cleared of stealing two pairs of her knickers. Funny how the crime he was cleared of, tended to stick in people's memories.

Finally he was deselected.

THE VIRGIN QUEEN

The Virgin Queen and her Porter

Margaret Hilda Thatcher, like the scientist Sir Isaac Newton (who died a virgin), was born in Grantham. Despite her thirteen years of unrivalled power, no hint of sexual scandal ever touched her.

Not that she wasn't sexy, Alan Clark famously remarked on her ankles, and Nicholas Fairbairn alleged that a Scottish Baronet had even propositioned her - but she kept her sexiness within her marriage. She didn't even write teasing love notes, unlike the Virgin Queen Elizabeth who famously wrote "Dear Frog" letters to a French admirer.

Perhaps, though, her greatest attribute on the bonking front was her lack of moral prudery. Many MPs who got into difficulty have attested to her support, from Cecil Parkinson at one end of the spectrum to Harvey Proctor at the other. At the 1987 General Election Harriet Crawley, then unmarried and pregnant, stood as a Tory Candidate in Brent East against "Red" Ken Livingstone - she also got Margaret Thatcher's support.

There is though one blemish on Margaret's copy-book - she never made Profumo a life peer. Since Profumo was hounded from office after the Keeler affair he has spent a considerable amount of time on welfare work in the East End of London, particularly at Toynbee Hall. Harold Wilson recognised this when he recommended him for a C.B.E. which Profumo received in 1975. With his wide range of experience and knowledge of social issues Profumo's contribution in the Lords would be considerable. Given Dennis Thatcher's acquaintance with Mandy Rice-Davies (q.v.) Margaret couldn't have forgotten Profumo and really should have put him in Lords - she should, shouldn't she.

A BEVY OF BEAUTIES

Minx and Max

PAMELLA BORDES

Pamella Bordes started life as Pamela Singh, and after being crowned Miss India, travelled via Hollywood to London. After mixing in the right circles she secured a job as research assistant to David Shaw MP, which enabled her to get a House of Commons Security Pass.

She was escorted to all the right places by a number of powerful men. She was even photographed out with the diminutive Minister of Sport, Colin Moynihan, at the Tory Winter Ball. (Colin eventually became Lord Moynihan after the death of his half-brother who had fled to the Philippines to avoid a fraud charge and spent the rest of his life running brothels in Manila, marrying ladies, and siring children, but not in an organised enough way that any of them managed to inherit the title.)

Then in March 1989 the News of the World struck. There were two problems with Pamella. The first was that she was earning money on the side as a call-girl. Some suggested £500-£2000 per night. The second was that she was close friends with a Major in the Libyan Security Service who just happened to be a cousin of Colonel Gadaffi.

Initially the Opposition thought they had a Profumo affair on their hands and whooped with glee, but times had changed.

Anyway, the Minister for Sport was hardly in a security position and no-one suggested that Colin Moynihan ever slept with her.

Max Clifford reportedly secured her £150,000 for her story. Christine Keeler's £23,000 for her story in 1963 was worth £167,000 in 1989 money, so it was roughly the right price. Then Pamella faded from view.

LADY BUCK

In early 1994 a doubtless apocryphal story was doing the rounds at London dinner parties. A woman at a party asks Jack Nicholson if he would like a dance. He replies "Wrong Verb". With Lady Buck it was more a case of wrong consonant.

Born Beinvenida Perez-Blanco and reportedly 32 in early March 1994 (she aged 5 years the following week) she had married Tory MP Sir Anthony Buck, a Navy Minister, in 1990. He was then 61 and she 28 (or maybe 33). They divorced in 1993.

She reportedly had many affairs including one with the Italian who masterminded the £60 million Knightsbridge safe robbery in 1986 and inevitably another with an Arab (an Iraqi). But the affair which brought her to the attention of the

Press was with Defence Chief Sir Peter Harding. She was worried about the security implications after the affair ended (although not, apparently, before or during the affair). So, off to Max Clifford and the News of the World.

There followed the inevitable sexy military puns. No doubt if Sir Peter had been an accountant it would all have been about double entry and verifying physical assets. Instead it was Tornados, Exocet missiles and something called Yellow Pages, possibly a reference to Chinese Female Naval Cadets.

Lady Buck collected a reported £75,000 and Sir Peter resigned, probably wondering at the hypocrisy of modern day morality. It was alright for Lord Nelson, and the Duke of Wellington even shared a mistress with Napoleon. But in these post cold-war, peace dividend times there might have been Security implications. I wish him well.

ANTONIA DE SANCHA

Antonia de Sancha was a 31 year old, six foot, half Spanish, half Swedish actress who had been to a private school and then R.A.D.A. The Press delighted in the fact that she had played a one-legged hooker in an avante garde film called The Pieman, in which she had sex with the Pizza delivery boy. In truth her career was not exactly blooming when she met David Mellor.

She didn't exactly kiss and tell but when her landlord's tape recordings were published that was the end of the affair. Dumped and penniless she sensibly met Max Clifford and sold her version to the press.

Among the claims she made about David Mellor:-

- he once made love to her is his Chelsea football kit.
- he recited Shakespeare to her in the nude.
- he liked to be spanked and have his toes sucked.

David Mellor denied all this but it's very difficult for a former lover to successfully squash such rumours, especially if they contain a brand name such as Chelsea kit or Mars Bars. Somehow the brand name makes it all believable.

The only way out is either to have lots of lovers, (so that another can deny it) or to debase it. "Goodness me, I save the Chelsea kit for my wife - the kit I used for her was Scunthorpe Reserves" might have worked.

MANDY RICE-DAVIES

There were four girls who gave evidence at the trial of the osteopath Stephen Ward who had introduced Keeler to Profumo and who was charged with living off the earnings of prostitution. Christine Keeler everybody knows about because she had the affair with Profumo. But there was also Vikki Barrett, the Miss Whiplash of the affair who charged £1 a stroke which would be about £10 today, and also Margaret Ricardo. But the most interesting character was Mandy Rice-Davies.

In fact Mandy Rice-Davies only knew Christine Keeler for four months but, as she has pointed out, their names are now (wrongly) stuck together in the public's mind like Crosse & Blackwell (or Raffles & Lamont q.v., or Chelsea kit & Mellor q.v., etc, etc.)

It was Mandy Rice-Davies who, when it was put to her that Lord Astor said her evidence was lies, replied with that memorable phrase:- "He would, wouldn't he". In 1966 she married an El Al steward and went to live in Israel where she started a highly successful Chinese Restaurant and Mandy's Disco. When he started playing around she left him and after a short marriage to the manager of her restaurant returned to London and lived comfortably off her restaurant earnings.

Eventually she married Ken Foreman who runs the public company Attwoods Plc, a company where Dennis Thatcher, wife of The Virgin Queen q.v. was Deputy Chairman.

As she once remarked "My life has been one long descent into respectability."

Horace Brand Farquhar - 1st Earl Farquhar
ex MP Marylebone West & Tory Party Treasurer 1922
Notorious Gay Embezzler

GAY YOUNG BACHELORS?

A small percentage of the population (5% - 10%) is homosexual so it would be surprising if no MPs were homosexuals.

Luckily we don't have to be surprised. More than a few are. But except for the admirable exception of the Islington Labour MP, Chris Smith, none have gone out of their way to admit it.

In the past this was understandable. The Criminal Law Amendment Act of 1885 made male homosexuality a crime. (Lesbianism has never been a crime but no MP has ever admitted to it) Buggery had been illegal for centuries and indeed was a capital offence until 1861 as the Earl of Castlehaven found out when he lost his head in 1633. So, from 1885 to the legalisation of homosexuality in 1967, male MPs who were homosexual had a problem. If they were caught they would face expulsion from the Commons plus a possible term in jail.

Inevitably there were scandals. It was strongly rumoured that Lord Rosebury, who became the Liberal Prime Minister in 1894, had an affair with the elder brother of Lord Alfred

Douglas - Oscar Wilde's boyfriend. Before the Second World War the Liberal Peers Lord Harcourt (committed suicide in 1922), and Earl Beauchamp (fled abroad in 1931) and the Tory Peer Lord Farquhar, were all involved in homosexual scandals.

In the 1950's the Labour MP William Field (public lavatories) and Tory MP Ian Harvey (guardsman in St James's Park) were convicted, although Lord Boothby who famously had a long affair with Harold Macmillan's wife managed to avoid prosecution for his gay affairs, as did Tom Driberg a notoriously promiscuous gay Labour MP.

Once the law had been changed, though, MPs of all political persuasions seem to have remained in their closets until prised out. This is silly. If we ignore a musicians sexual orientation when we buy their records would we not ignore a Politician's sexual orientation when we vote. Chris Smith thought so and was proved right. Maybe the others should be more open.

DR KEITH HAMPSON.

TORY MP
Leeds North-West

In 1984 Dr Keith Hampson, who was at the time a happily married PPS to Michael Heseltine, the then Defence Minister, was charged with indecently assaulting a plain clothes male policeman in a homosexual club in Soho called the Gay Theatre.What was Dr Hampson doing there ? Apparently he had some spare time and went there out of curiosity. What the police were doing there if not acting as agents provocateurs is another question.

In the event the jury failed to reach a decision so he was acquitted. In 1984 the public were far more inclined to believe police witnesses. It seems highly unlikely that a case such as this would be brought today. Dr Hampson remains an M.P. but his career seems to have stalled.

ALLAN ROBERTS
ex LABOUR MP
Bootle

In 1980 Allan Roberts was reported to have been found cavorting in a Berlin nightclub. Apparently he was dressed in an S.S. uniform and was being led around in a dog-collar whilst being whipped.

Then there were allegations of sex offences with teenage youths in 1983. “I’m not the least bit bothered”, he was quoted as saying. “I’ve had to put up with this sort of thing all through my political career”.

Then there was the Bethnal Green pub "The Lord Hood" he bought in the summer of 1986 and turned into a gay pub. It became famous for selling House of Commons claret before he sold it in December 1987.

HARVEY PROCTOR
ex TORY MP
Billericay

Harvey was a right-wing, anti-immigration Conservative MP who was once reported as saying:- "Each Asian admitted for settlement means two or more additional Asians within a few years".

Unhappily his fears of little brown people under the beds became reality in 1987 when allegations began to appear of a naked Arab boy found under his bed whilst he was staying in a Moroccan Hotel. At least the bed was in Morocco, not England, so maybe all was O.K.

Then there was the rather alarming report of an art dealer being found naked except for a pair of underpants at 3 a.m. one morning outside his flat in Fulham. Nobody reported the make of underpants but it was probably normal attire for Fulham.

From shirtlifter to shirtshifter

Unfortunately in May 1987 he decided not to seek reselection after being fined £1,450 for spanking rent boys at his Fulham flat. Apparently one of his favourite games was to play Trivial Pursuits. Each time a rent boy got a question wrong he would get another whack with a cane. As Cynthia Payne, the convicted brothel keeper, pointed out "If he was caught spanking a woman he'd have got off Scot free". This was true, as none of the rent boys were under 17.

After leaving the Commons he set up a shirt shop in Richmond in which many of his fellow MPs invested. Michael Heseltine and Jeffrey Archer were reported as having invested £5,000 each, Mr Archer commenting "I don't think the best thing to do when someone is down is to kick them" Spanking yes, kicking no.

The shop flourishes - even John Major apparently has shirts from it. But it's not always safe, as poor Neil Hamilton, a Tory Trade Minister, found in July 1992 when the shop was raided by "gay bashers" as he was buying a shirt. Neil ended up with a broken nose - perhaps he should have spent the day playing Happy Families at home, or joined Keith Best q.v. and played Tiddliwinks.

MATTHEW PARRIS
ex TORY MP
West Derbyshire

During Matthew's time as M.P. he kept his gayness out of the Press but apparently enjoyed the thrill of possible exposure. This almost happened one time when he met a Parliamentary journalist in a gay London pub. Luckily the journalist was not there on business.

Now a Times columnist, he reckons that considerably more than 10% of MPs have homosexual tendencies but that he has never had an affair with any of them "Golly..... one can do better". Quite so!

JEREMY THORPE
ex LIBERAL MP
Devon North

In 1978 Jeremy Thorpe, a former leader of the Liberal Party was charged with conspiracy to murder his former friend - a male model called Norman Scott. Scott claimed to have had a homosexual relationship with Thorpe which Thorpe consistently denied, although his defence counsel Peter Taylor Q.C. did acknowledge that Jeremy Thorpe had had homosexual tendencies at one time

The case arose after a former airline-pilot Andrew Newton was arrested for shooting Scott's dog Rinka and attempting to murder Scott, who was allegedly blackmailing him over nude photos. Newton was convicted in 1976 and jailed for two years.

Later Newton, Scott and Peter Bessell (a former Liberal M.P.) appeared for the prosecution alleging that Thorpe had tried to hire someone to kill Scott, to stop Scott blackmailing Thorpe.

In the event Jeremy Thorpe and his co-defendents were all acquitted. However the publicity cost him the leadership of the Liberal Party and his political career.

CARRY ON IN THE CABINET

During 1993 and 1994 rumours begun to emerge that at least two Cabinet Ministers were involved in homosexual orgies.

Tricia Howard who was Paddy Pantsdown's mistress for five months in 1987, revealed that certain Ministers had dressed up as French maids and acted obscenely. The gay footballer Justin Fashanu was also revealed to be trying to sell his story of three in a bed sex romps with two senior government members. Who were they? Who cares? (ie I know who has been named, but do you think I can afford to say ?)

Spot the ass

THE MORAL OF THE STORY

GEORGE WIGG
ex LABOUR MP
Dudley

I started with John Profumo and, in a way, I'll end with him. The Labour MP George Wigg was by all accounts not a particularly pleasant person. It was his question to Profumo q.v. which prompted the statement in which Profumo lied to Parliament.

Some thirteen years later in December 1976, the by then Lord Wigg of Dudley appeared in court charged with insulting behaviour. The police had picked him up kerb-crawling in Mayfair but kerb-crawling was not then a criminal offence. Lord Wigg's insistence that he was just looking for early editions of the next day's newspapers was not believed by the Magistrate, but he was acquitted of insulting behaviour.

Nine years later in 1985 the Tory MP. Janet Fookes introduced a Private Member's Bill to make kerb-crawling a crime. At first it was filibustered by Matthew Parris q.v., but eventually it passed.

It seems to me that the kerb-crawling Bill is a typical example of the moral hypocrisy and stupidity of politicians. Prostitution like drugs will always be with us. Why not legalise brothels and tax them ? Such Acts of Parliament, like the 1885 Act which made male homosexuality a crime, achieve very little except lives being destroyed and police time being wasted.

Maybe if MPs were more open about what actually happens and attempted to foster a more liberal morality, they would find less interest being taken in their own little sexual mishaps. Hopefully the single-mother bashing episode of the Back to Basics morality campaign has backfired sufficiently to teach them this, but I doubt it.

Alert readers will notice that I have omitted a number of Politicians who have died in unfortunate circumstances:- Lord Avon, Cadbury, Stephen Milligan and the Caithness saga. Such personal tragedies have no place in a humour book but it is worth noting that personal tragedy is not the highest price paid for moral double standards.

The highest price is the tragedy and mess suffered by the people of Northern Ireland. Had Parnell's affair with Katie O'Shea not caused such a scandal it is possible that a United Ireland would have succeeded in getting home rule a century ago.

Maybe the French have a better understanding of these things. At the time of the Parkinson scandal President Mitterand commented "If I had to select my Cabinet with such restrictions placed on me, I would only have forty homosexuals left to choose from!" But then again, the use of the word "only" lets him down.

Alan Clark
ex Tory MP Plymouth (Sutton)
Historian, Politician, Diarist and Bonker

ADDENDUM

One of the problems in writing this book is that the Politicians won't do the decent thing and stop Bonking for a few months. Even as this book was going to press, The News of the World published allegations linking Michael Brown, the Tory MP for Brigg and Cleethorpes and Tory Whip, to under-age gay sex. Michael denied these reports and resigned his Government job to fight them.

In his excellent and very funny diaries, Alan Clark records an amusing story about Derek Lord, a gay self-assured black companion of Michael Brown. Apparently one of Michael Brown's rough Derbyshire farmer constituents remarked of Derek:-

"Eee that twat's dad moost've eaten a posh missionary" - They're not exactly politically correct in Derbyshire.

The rest of this page, and the next, I have left blank. No doubt the MPs will fill them up very quickly.

Norman ffamily-Values

For goodness sake what have I done to be tortured like this. Do you think the New Testament could ever have been completed if Christ had behaved like some demented Jack-in-the-Box and kept popping back every five minutes for another Resurrection ?

I had just paid off Norman ffamily-Values and collected the final picture from the wondrous Charlotte, when peekaboo it's Alan Clark. Rather a lot of peekaboo in actualitee.

Alan Clark was a Tory Arms Procurement Minister under The Virgin Queen and it appears he allowed the title to go to his nether regions. Not only did he procure the arms of a judge's wife but the arms of both her daughters as well.

In his Diaries he mentions them all by name but, to be fair, he never specifically says he bedded any of them. (The entry on page nine of his book can be read either way) However the mother and one daughter decided to spill the beans (News of the World, Max Clifford, usual humbug, you know the scene.) Why did they do it? Max's reported remark summed it up best. "It's all about revenge and money - the usual combination." Probably Alan Clark had the last laugh as sales of his book doubtless increased and his wife knew anyway.

O.K. That's it. Now will all you Tory MPs please keep it in your trousers, at least for a month or so. Please!

Farquhar McNaughty

McNaughty Books are available from all good Book and Gift shops, or direct from the publishers John Napir Ltd at P O Box 3353, London N1 - 1SR at £4.99 per copy.